Copyright ©Anna C. Mcginley
All relevant Reserved
This book's content cannot be reproduced, stored, or transmitted in any form without the copyright owner's permission. This includes electronic or mechanical means, photocopying, recording, or any other method.

FOREX FOR ALL TRADINGS WITH METHODS FOR ALL STAGES

Includes MT4 and MT5 ELUCIDATION

Anna C. Mcginley

Table of Contents

1. About the Book

2. Introduction

3. Chapter 1
Understanding the Basics of Forex
Understanding the Basics of Forex

What is Forex?

Key Players in the Forex Market

Currency Pairs and How They Work

4. Chapter 2:
Getting Started in Forex Trading
Getting Started in Forex Trading

Setting Up a Trading Account

Choosing a Broker

Understanding the Trading Platform

5. Chapter 3:
Forex Terminology for Beginners
Forex Terminology for Beginners

Pips, Lots, and Leverage

Bid and Ask Prices

Spread and Commission

6. Chapter 4

Analyzing the Forex Market
 Analyzing the Forex Market

Fundamental Analysis

Technical Analysis

Market Sentiment Analysis

7. Chapter 5:

Introduction to Trading Strategies.
Developing a Trading Strategy

Types of Forex Trading Strategies

Setting Goals and Risk Management

Creating a Trading Plan

8. Chapter 6:

The Psychology of Forex Trading

The Psychology of Forex Trading

Emotional Control in Trading

Common Psychological Traps

Building a Winning Mindset

9. Chapter 7:

Risk Management Essentials
Risk Management Essentials

Importance of Stop-Loss and Take-Profit Orders

Calculating Risk-Reward Ratios

Position Sizing and Money Management

10. Chapter 8:

Forex Trading Tools and Resources
Forex Trading Tools and Resources

Essential Tools for Forex Traders

Recommended Books, Courses, and Websites

11. Chapter 9:

Forex for Beginners – A Step-by-Step Guide

Forex for Beginners: A Step-by-Step Guide

Practical Exercises and Demos

Avoiding Common Beginner Mistakes

12. Chapter 10:

Advanced Forex Trading Techniques

Advanced Forex Trading Techniques

Using Indicators and Oscillators

Advanced Chart Patterns

Algorithmic and Automated Trading

13. Chapter 11:

Case Studies and Real-Life Examples
Case Studies and Real-Life Examples

Success Stories in Forex Trading

Lessons from Mistakes

14. Chapter 12:

Future Trends in Forex Trading
Future Trends in Forex Trading

Emerging Markets and Cryptocurrency in Forex

AI and Machine Learning in Forex

15. CHAPTER 13
Final Thoughts and Upcoming Actions for Your Forex Adventure.
Final Thoughts and Upcoming Actions for Your Forex Adventure
15. Conclusion and Next Steps

About the Book

"Forex Easy Money Making" is a comprehensive guide designed for those new to forex trading and experienced traders seeking a structured approach to profit-making. The book combines foundational knowledge with practical strategies and insights into market behavior, aiming to transform beginners into informed traders and guide advanced users toward maximizing their trading efficiency.

Readers will gain an understanding of both the technical and psychological aspects of trading. By providing accessible terminology, real-life examples, and actionable steps, this book demystifies the forex market and makes money-making methods approachable for all levels. "Forex Easy Money Making" stands as a valuable resource, ready to serve as both a beginner's guide and an ongoing reference for successful trading.

Introduction

Forex, or the foreign exchange market, represents the world's largest financial marketplace, where trillions of dollars are traded daily. Its appeal lies in its accessibility, potential for profitability, and the sheer dynamism of currency movements. Yet, despite the allure, forex trading can be challenging, particularly for those without a firm understanding of market mechanics and trading psychology.

In this book, we start with the basics, ensuring readers understand core concepts such as currency pairs, the function of a trading platform, and the crucial role of analysis in decision-making. From there, we'll explore various trading strategies, risk management practices, and delve into more complex subjects like automated trading and psychological resilience. This approach ensures that even readers with no prior experience can progress confidently into the forex world.

Whether your goal is to create a consistent income stream or to gain an edge in an unpredictable market, "Forex Easy Money Making" provides the tools, techniques, and guidance necessary to navigate and succeed in forex trading.

Chapter 1

Understanding the Basics of Forex

What is Forex?

The foreign exchange market, often referred to as "forex" or "FX," is a global decentralized platform for buying, selling, and exchanging currencies. Unlike stock exchanges, which are centralized, forex operates 24 hours a day across various international markets. This continuous nature allows currencies to be traded globally, across different time zones, making it a dynamic and accessible market for all types of traders.

The forex market facilitates global trade, allowing businesses to buy goods and services in different currencies, investors to hedge against currency risks, and speculators to make profits by predicting currency movements. The immense volume of daily transactions, reaching over $7.5

trillion, makes forex the most liquid market in the world.

Key Players in the Forex Market

Several key participants play a role in forex, each contributing to its liquidity and volatility. Understanding these participants can offer insights into market movements and trading strategies:

Central Banks: Central banks, like the Federal Reserve or the European Central Bank, play a significant role in forex. They manage currency supply, set interest rates, and implement monetary policies that impact currency values. For example, when a central bank raises interest rates, its currency generally strengthens.

Financial Institutions and Banks: Commercial and investment banks engage in substantial forex trading, providing liquidity and making profits through exchange rates. They often serve clients like corporations and hedge funds but also engage in proprietary trading to gain from currency fluctuations.

Corporations: Multinational companies trading across borders often engage in forex to hedge against currency risks. For instance, a company importing goods from a foreign country may buy that currency to secure a stable cost, avoiding fluctuations that could increase expenses.

Hedge Funds and Investment Managers: These entities trade forex to diversify their portfolios or generate profits. Hedge funds may engage in high-risk trades by leveraging large amounts of capital, making them influential players in the forex market.

Retail Traders: Individual traders, often using online trading platforms, make up a smaller but growing part of the forex market. Retail traders aim to profit from exchange rate fluctuations, often relying on technical analysis and trading strategies suited to their financial goals.

Currency Pairs and How They Work

Forex trading is always about two currencies, called currency pairs.

The pair represents the exchange rate between two currencies, indicating how much of the quoted currency (second currency) is needed to buy one unit of the base currency (first currency).

1. **Major Pairs**: Major pairs include currencies from large economies, like EUR/USD (Euro/US Dollar), GBP/USD (British Pound/US Dollar), and USD/JPY (US Dollar/Japanese Yen). These pairs are highly liquid and often have lower transaction costs, making them popular for all traders.

2. **Minor Pairs:** Also known as cross-currency pairs, minors don't involve the USD, such as EUR/GBP (Euro/British Pound) or AUD/JPY (Australian Dollar/Japanese Yen). Though they have lower liquidity than major pairs, they are often favored by experienced traders seeking volatility.

3. **Exotic Pairs**: Exotic pairs involve currencies from emerging or smaller economies, like USD/TRY (US Dollar/Turkish Lira) or EUR/HKD (Euro/Hong Kong Dollar). While they offer high-profit potential, exotic pairs are less liquid and more volatile, carrying higher risk.

How Currency Prices are Determined

The value of a currency pair fluctuates based on supply and demand, influenced by economic indicators, geopolitical events, and market sentiment. Key factors include:

Interest Rates: Bigger interests attract foreign capital, increasing the level of demand for a currency.

Central banks adjusting rates can significantly impact exchange rates.

<u>Inflation Rates:</u> Low inflation typically strengthens a currency, while high inflation decreases purchasing power and may devalue the currency.

<u>Economic Indicators</u>: Reports like GDP growth, employment rates, and manufacturing indices reflect a country's economic health and can drive currency value.

<u>Political Stability</u>: Political events, such as elections, policies, or international conflicts, often cause volatility. Currencies of politically

stable countries are usually more desirable.

The Role of Brokers in Forex Trading

Brokers act as intermediaries, providing a trading platform for retail traders. Most brokers offer leverage, allowing traders to control larger positions with smaller initial investments. While leverage amplifies profit potential, it also heightens risk, making it essential for traders to manage leverage responsibly.

Types of brokers

Market Makers: These brokers "make the market" by setting bids and asking prices, potentially trading against their clients.

Electronic Communication Network (ECN) Brokers:
ECN brokers connect traders directly to the interbank market, ensuring transparent pricing and typically lower spreads.

Why Forex is Different from Other Financial Markets

Forex is unique in its accessibility, liquidity, and flexibility. Unlike stocks or commodities, forex trading is continuous, allowing traders to respond to market events in real-time. The high liquidity means trades can be executed quickly, reducing slippage risk, and providing ample opportunities for those seeking short- or long-term gains.

Additionally, forex offers various trading styles, from day trading to swing trading and even algorithmic trading, catering to different trader profiles. The ability to go long or short on currency pairs without restrictions further adds to forex's appeal as a flexible investment vehicle.

Summary of Chapter 1

This chapter establishes the fundamental understanding of forex, emphasizing its role in global finance, key participants, and factors influencing currency values. With a grasp of these essentials, readers will be prepared to navigate the forex market, recognize its unique features, and appreciate the complexities of trading currency pairs. This foundational knowledge is crucial as we delve into the practicalities of starting in forex trading, covered in the following chapters.

Chapter 2

Getting Started in Forex Trading

Setting Up a Trading Account

Before diving into forex trading, the first step is to set up a trading account with a broker. The broker serves as the intermediary between the trader and the market, providing access to trading platforms and tools.

Select a Broker: choosing the right broker is very important
. Look for brokers who are regulated by financial authorities, as they are more likely to operate transparently. Consider aspects like customer support, transaction fees, leverage options, and available currency pairs.

Account Types: Many brokers offer different account types, such as standard, mini, and micro accounts.

These vary in minimum deposits and trading sizes, so beginners may prefer micro or mini accounts to start with smaller capital requirements.

The setup process usually involves verifying your identity, submitting documents (such as a passport or utility bill), and funding your account through bank transfer, credit card, or e-wallet.

Choosing a Broker

Finding a reliable broker is critical for success in forex trading.

There are some good factors to choose when talking about a broker:

Regulation and Security: Regulated brokers operate under the supervision of authorities like the U.S. the Australian Securities and Investments Commission (ASIC), the Commodity Futures Trading Commission (CFTC), or the Financial Conduct Authority (FCA) in the United Kingdom. Strict rules are enforced by these regulatory agencies to safeguard merchants.

Fees and Spreads: Brokers make money through spreads (the difference between the bid and ask prices) or commissions. Compare fees across brokers, as high fees can cut into profits.

While some brokers offer fixed spreads, others have variable spreads that change based on the state of the market.

Leverage and Margin: Leverage allows traders to control larger positions with a small amount of capital, amplifying both potential gains and losses. Understand your broker's leverage offerings and ensure you are comfortable with the associated risks.

Platform and Tools: The trading platform should be user-friendly and offer the necessary features, such as charts, analysis tools, and news feeds. Popular platforms like MetaTrader 4 (MT4) or MetaTrader 5 (MT5) offer a robust suite of tools for beginners and experienced traders alike.

Understanding the Trading Platform

The trading platform is where all transactions and analysis happen. Familiarizing yourself with the platform will make it easier to execute trades effectively. Most platforms, like MT4 or MT5, include the following features:

Order Types: Platforms typically support various order types, including market orders (immediate execution at the current price) and pending orders like limit and stop orders (executed when price reaches a specified level).

Charts and Indicators: Platforms offer charts and technical indicators, such as moving averages, RSI (Relative Strength Index), and MACD (Moving Average Convergence Divergence), to help traders analyze trends and make informed decisions.

Account Information: Traders can monitor their account balance, equity, and margin levels. Keeping an eye on these metrics is crucial for managing risk and avoiding margin calls.

Mobile Compatibility: Many trading platforms are available on mobile devices, allowing traders to monitor and execute trades on the go. This flexibility is beneficial for traders who need to stay connected to the market at all times.

Starting with a Demo Account

One of the best ways to practice and gain confidence is to start with a demo account. Most brokers offer demo accounts that allow traders to trade with virtual money while experiencing real market conditions.

Test Trading Strategies: Without risking real money, traders can experiment with various strategies and refine their approach.

Understand Market Movements: Demo accounts let traders observe how different economic events impact currency prices, helping them develop a better feel for the market.

Gain Platform Proficiency: Operating a demo account allows users to learn the features of the trading platform without making costly mistakes in a live environment.

Building a Trading Plan

A trading plan serves as a roadmap for achieving success in forex. It should define goals, risk tolerance, and trading strategies. A solid trading plan can help you stay disciplined and avoid impulsive decisions. Key components include:

Setting Goals: Clarify your objectives, whether it's to create a steady income, accumulate wealth, or just learn the market.

You'll stay motivated if your goals are attainable and realistic.

Defining Risk Tolerance: Determine the amount of capital you're willing to risk on each trade, typically a small percentage of your account balance (often around 1-2%).

Selecting a Strategy: Decide on the strategy you will use, such as scalping (short-term trades), day trading, or swing trading (longer-term trades). Each strategy requires different skill levels and time commitments.

Common Mistakes to Avoid as a Beginner

Entering the forex market can be overwhelming, and many beginners fall into common traps.

By being aware of these mistakes, you can steer clear of expensive ones:

Over-leveraging: Using excessive leverage increases the size of trades relative to your account balance.

Even though leverage might increase earnings, it can also increase losses.

Avoid high leverage, especially as a beginner.

Lack of Discipline: Emotions can cloud judgment, leading to impulsive decisions.
Follow your trading strategy and refrain from "revenge trading" in order to promptly recover losses.

Ignoring Risk Management: Setting stop-loss orders can prevent small losses from becoming large ones.
Risk management is very important for long-term profitability.

Chasing Losses: Trying to recover a loss by making larger trades often leads to further losses. Accepting losses as part of the learning process can help maintain a balanced mindset.

Starting Small and Scaling Up

As a beginner, it's wise to start with small trades. Focus on learning the market, refining your trading strategy, and building confidence. Here are some tips to help you scale up gradually:

Trade with Minimal Risk: Begin with a micro or mini account to trade smaller lot sizes. This approach reduces risk while allowing you to build experience.

Set Daily/Weekly Limits: Limit the amount of capital you're willing to risk per day or week, and avoid trading during times of high emotion or fatigue.

Gradual Scaling: As you gain confidence and consistency, you can increase the trade size and explore more complex strategies. Gradual scaling also helps prevent emotional burnout and ensures steady learning.

Chapter 3

Forex Terminology for Beginners

Leverage, Lots, and 1 Pip Managing deals and determining possible gains or losses require an understanding of the fundamental units of forex trading. Below is a list of terms that are frequently used: The smallest price change in a currency pair is called a pip (percentage in point), and for the majority of currency pairs, it is usually the fourth decimal place (e.g., 0.0001). Pips are essential for determining profit or loss since they quantify price movements. For example, EUR/USD has moved 50 pips if it goes from 1.1200 to 1.1250. Lot: Standardized units of currency, or lots, are used in forex trading. There are three primary lot sizes: 100,000 units of the base currency make up the standard lot. 10,000 units make up the mini lot. Micro Lot: One thousand pieces. In order to properly limit risk, beginners frequently begin with micro or mini lots. Leverage: With less capital, traders can manage bigger bets thanks to leverage. With a 1:100 leverage, for instance, you may manage a $10,000 deal with just $100. Leverage can improve profits, but it also raises the possibility of losses, thus risk management is essential.

Asking and Bidding Prices.

The bid and the ask are the two prices that are used in the currency market. The price at which the market is willing to purchase a pair of currencies is known as the bid. The bid price is what you sell when you sell a currency pair. The price at which the market is prepared to sell a pair of currencies is known as the ask price. A currency pair is purchased at the asking price. The spread, which stands for the cost of the trade, is the difference between the bid and ask prices. For instance, the spread is 2 pips if the EUR/USD bid is 1.1200 and the ask is 1.1202.

Commission and Spread

The difference between the ask and bid prices is known as the spread, and it serves as the broker's payment for executing the trade. The volatility of currency pairs, liquidity, and broker type are some of the variables that affect spread sizes. **Fixed Spread:** Regardless of the state of the market, certain brokers offer fixed spreads, which maintain the same gap between the bid and ask prices. Variable Spread: The difference in a variable spread varies according to the volatility and liquidity of the market. Wider spreads are frequently the result of high volatility.

In lieu of or in addition to a spread, some brokers charge a commission. Brokers that provide raw market spreads frequently impose commissions, which are typically computed as a tiny fraction of the trade size.

Margin Call and Margin

The sum of money required by a trader to initiate a leveraged position is known as the margin. It basically functions as a security deposit that lets traders borrow money from the broker. Initial Margin: The amount of money needed to start a trade. For instance, a $100 margin is needed to open a $10,000 position with 1:100 leverage.

Margin Call: The broker may issue a margin call if a trader has losses that cause their account balance to drop below a certain threshold. In order to reach the necessary margin, the trader must either cancel positions or make more deposits. It is crucial to comprehend margin and margin calls since trading without enough margin may require positions to be liquidated, which could result in large losses.

Take-Profit and Stop-Loss Orders

Take-profit and stop-loss orders are essential instruments for controlling risk and guaranteeing profits. A stop-loss order limits possible losses by instructing a trade to automatically close when it hits a predetermined level.

If you buy EUR/USD at 1.1200 and set a stop-loss at 1.1150, for instance, your trade will automatically shut if the price falls to 1.1150, limiting additional loss. Take-Profit Order: A take-profit order instructs a trade to be automatically closed when it hits a predetermined profit threshold. For example, if you start a trade at 1.1200 and set a take-profit at 1.1250, the transaction will automatically cancel when the price hits 1.1250, protecting your gains. Without continual oversight, these orders assist traders in adhering to their trading strategies, safeguarding gains and reducing losses.

Long and Short Positions

A crucial aspect of trading is comprehending long and short positions.

Long Position: Going long means buying a currency pair, expecting the base currency to appreciate against the quote currency. For example, if you go long on EUR/USD at 1.1200, you believe the euro will strengthen relative to the dollar.

Short Position: Going short means selling a currency pair, anticipating that the base currency will depreciate against the quote currency. If you go short on EUR/USD at 1.1200, you expect the euro to weaken against the dollar.

Both positions allow traders to profit from market fluctuations, whether the currency is rising or falling in value.

Order Types: Market, Limit, and Stop Orders

Different order types give traders flexibility in entering and exiting trades:

Market Order: An order to buy or sell at the current market price. Market orders are executed immediately, ensuring quick entry or exit but not always guaranteeing a specific price due to slippage.

Limit Order: An order to buy or sell at a specified price or better. Limit orders provide more control over entry and exit points, but there's no guarantee they will be filled if the price doesn't reach the specified level.

Stop Order: A stop order becomes a market order once the price reaches a certain level. For instance, a buy stop order is placed above the current price, triggering a buy once the price rises to the stop level.

Understanding these order types helps traders plan entries and exits based on their strategies and market conditions.

Slippage and Liquidity

Slippage and liquidity impact trade execution and costs:

Slippage: Slippage occurs when a trade is executed at a different price than expected, often due to high volatility or low liquidity. For example, if you place a market order during a major news event, the price may shift before the order is filled, leading to slippage.

Liquidity: The ease of buying or selling an asset without changing its price is known as liquidity.

High liquidity means orders can be filled quickly with minimal price changes, while low liquidity may result in wider spreads and higher slippage.

Understanding Risk and Reward

Risk and reward are key factors in trading decisions. Evaluating potential risk versus potential profit helps traders set realistic goals and stay disciplined.

Risk-Reward Ratio: The risk-reward ratio compares the potential loss of a trade to its potential gain. For instance, if you risk 50 pips to gain

100 pips, the ratio is 1:2. Traders often aim for a minimum 1:2 ratio to ensure profitable trades.

Position Sizing: Proper position sizing controls the amount of risk in each trade. By calculating the position size based on risk tolerance and stop-loss distance, traders protect their capital while pursuing profitable opportunities.

Chapter 4

Analyzing the Forex Market

1 Overview of Market Analysis
To make wise trading selections, one must analyze the forex market. Sentiment analysis, technical

analysis, and fundamental analysis are the three main categories of analysis in forex. Every strategy offers distinct perspectives on market patterns, enabling traders to forecast price changes and recognize chances. A trader's chances of success can be greatly increased by knowing these strategies and when to use them. We'll examine each form of analysis in this chapter, emphasizing the instruments, methods, and approaches that forex traders frequently employ.

Basic Study

The economic, political, and social elements that affect currency prices are examined by fundamental analysis. Traders that view the market

from a macroeconomic perspective frequently choose this kind of analysis, which is crucial for comprehending long-term trends.
Economic Indicators: Important economic reports that provide light on a nation's economic health include GDP, retail sales, inflation rates, and employment statistics.

A robust GDP growth rate, for instance, indicates a sound economy and is likely to strengthen the value of the nation's currency.

Interest Rates: By implementing interest rate policies, central banks like the Federal Reserve and the European Central Bank affect the value of currencies. Higher interest rates typically draw in foreign capital, which raises the currency's demand. Geopolitical Events: Currency swings can result from political events like elections, trade deals, or hostilities. For example, perceived volatility caused by trade conflicts or uncertainty about the outcome of an election can devalue a currency. Statements on

Monetary Policy:
Central banks make announcements regarding their monetary policies on a regular basis. These declarations impact market sentiment and currency values by revealing future intentions about interest rates and other economic indicators. Because it offers a more comprehensive

understanding of market dynamics and economic health, fundamental analysis is frequently employed in conjunction with other techniques.

Technical Evaluation

Examining past price data and spotting trends to forecast future movements is known as technical analysis. This approach is very common among short-term traders since traders utilize charts and indicators to examine price movement. Price charts: Technical analysis is based on charts. Line charts, bar charts, and candlestick charts are common varieties; candlesticks are especially well-liked because of their capacity to provide comprehensive price data, including open, close, high, and low.

Technical traders search for patterns on charts that suggest potential future price movements. <u>*Typical designs consist*</u> of: A reversal pattern that signals a shift in the trend is the head and shoulders. Double Top/Bottom: Indicates possible reversals in trends. Triangles: Patterns of continuation or reversal are suggested by symmetrical, ascending, or descending triangles. Indicators: Indicators assist traders in determining volatility, momentum, and trends. Typical indications consist of: Price data is smoothed by moving averages (MA) to reveal trends. Combinations such as the 50-day and 200-day moving averages are frequently used by traders to validate trends. The Relative Strength Index (RSI) gauges how quickly and how much a price moves. RSI levels below 30 are considered oversold, while those exceeding 70 are generally considered overbought. Convergence of Moving Averages Divergence (MACD): By comparing moving averages, it illustrates shifts in momentum. Opportunities to purchase or sell may be indicated by crossovers between MACD lines. Technical analysis is a crucial tool for trade timing since it assists traders in determining entry and exit locations.

Sentiment Analysis

By measuring the market's mood, sentiment analysis assists traders in determining whether most traders are bearish (pessimistic) or bullish (optimistic) about a currency pair. Report on Commitment of Traders (COT): Published weekly by the Commodity Futures Trading Commission (CFTC), the COT report reveals the holdings held by different types of traders, including commercial and non-commercial traders. This report can show if a currency is oversold or overbought.

Retail Sentiment Indicators: Data indicating the proportion of retail traders with long or short positions on a currency pair is provided by some firms. An overbought situation, suggesting a possible reversal, may be indicated by a large proportion of traders holding long holdings.

News and Social Media: News headlines and social media trends also have an impact on market mood. Significant news events, such political shifts or the revelation of economic data, have the power to swiftly alter market mood and increase volatility. Since sentiment research offers a psychological viewpoint on the market, it is frequently combined with technical and fundamental analysis.

Combining Methods of Analysis
Even though each type of analysis has advantages, profitable traders frequently integrate sentiment, technical, and fundamental analysis to get a complete picture of the market. This is how they collaborate:

Fundamental Analysis for Long-Term Trends The best way to comprehend long-term trends is to look at fundamental elements like interest rates and economic indicators. For instance, a trader would search for long-term chances to purchase the USD if the Federal Reserve signals future rate hikes.

Timing with Technical Analysis: Technical analysis can be used to identify entry and exit points in relation to a more general fundamental trend. A trader with a long-term bullish outlook on EUR/USD, for example, would wait for a technical pattern to indicate the best time to enter the market. Confirmation Sentiment Analysis: Sentiment analysis supports the validity of trading judgments.

For instance, looking at bearish mood indicators might validate the trade's potential if a trader intends to short a currency pair based on technical and fundamental analysis. Combining these techniques enables traders to make well-informed, well-balanced judgments, improving their capacity to react to market swings.

Market Analysis Tools

To help traders analyze the forex market, there are a number of tools available:

Economic Calendars: These provide a list of forthcoming economic events and data releases, including interest rate announcements and GDP statistics. Traders can prepare for possible volatility with the use of these calendars. **Charting Platforms**: A range of technical analysis charting tools and indicators are available on platforms such as MetaTrader 4 (MT4) and TradingView. News Sources: Fundamental analysis requires keeping up with world events. Bloomberg, Reuters, and the financial news sections of respectable websites are examples of trustworthy sources.

Sentiment Indicators: A number of brokers and financial websites provide sentiment data that displays the proportion of retail traders in long and short positions. An overview of market mood is given by this data. By using these resources, traders can stay updated and make well-informed judgments on time.

Common Analysis Errors Analysis errors are common among novice traders and can result in bad trading choices.

The following typical pitfalls should be avoided: Over-reliance on a Single Analysis Type: An insufficient understanding of the market may result from relying only on one method. In general, a well-rounded strategy that incorporates all three forms of analysis works better.

Ignoring Risk Management: Analysis alone does not ensure success. One way to guard against unanticipated market movements is to use stop-loss and take-profit orders.

Chasing News Events: Because of the extreme volatility and erratic price fluctuations, trading right after a significant news release can be dangerous. Usually, it's best to wait for the market to calm down before acting.

Excessive analysis: Also referred to as "analysis paralysis," excessive analysis might result in lost chances. This problem can be avoided by developing and following a systematic trading strategy.

CHAPTER 5

Introduction to Trading Strategies.

An organized plan for making trades based on predetermined standards and market research is called a trading strategy. Reducing emotional decision-making and attaining consistency require a well-thought-out plan. Entry and exit points, position sizes, risk management guidelines, and performance evaluation techniques are all specified in a well-written strategy. From short-term to long-term methods, we will examine a variety of trading strategies in this chapter and offer advice on how to develop, test, and improve a strategy that fits your objectives and risk tolerance.

Forex Trading Strategy Types

Various trading techniques, periods, and risk profiles are best suited for different tactics.

Here are a few typical tactics:
Making several transactions in a single day in order to profit from

slight price fluctuations is known as scalping.

Scalpers typically hold positions for a few seconds to minutes and depend on low spreads and high liquidity. This method calls for self-control, fast decision-making, and a solid grasp of technical analysis.

Day Trading: The goal of day trading is to take advantage of brief price swings by initiating and terminating trades inside a single trading day. Technical analysis and current affairs are used by day traders to inform their choices.

Day trading typically entails fewer deals and marginally longer holding periods than scalping. Swing Trading: In order to profit from more significant price moves, or "swings," swing traders hold their holdings for a few days to weeks. Swing traders enter trades during retracements and hold until the trend returns. They do this by using both technical and fundamental analysis to detect trends. A long-term strategy, position trading involves traders holding positions for weeks, months, or even years.

This approach, which focuses on economic developments, interest rate fluctuations, and geopolitical events, mostly uses fundamental analysis. By minimizing short-term volatility, position traders seek to profit from significant changes in the value of the currency. Identifying and trading in the direction of a persistent trend is the goal of trend-following methods. In order to enter positions that are in accordance with the trend and hold them until signals point to a reversal, traders utilize indicators such as trend lines or moving averages.

The concept of range trading is predicated on the notion that prices fluctuate between levels of support and resistance within a range. Range traders use technical analysis to determine entry and exit points, buying at support and selling at resistance. This approach works well in sideways, stable markets. Every approach has different requirements for technical expertise, risk tolerance, and time. Selecting a strategy that fits your lifestyle, level of experience, and financial objectives is crucial.

Goal-Setting and Risk Control.

Without specific objectives and risk management procedures, a strategy cannot be considered successful. While risk management safeguards your money, goal-setting aids in tracking progress and keeping focus. Establish explicit goals, whether they are performance-based (like increasing win rate) or financial (like reaching a particular return). Objectives ought to be time-bound, quantifiable, and reasonable.

Assess your risk tolerance to see how much risk you can tolerate in each trade and in general. In order to sustain a series of losses without exhausting their cash, many traders risk between one and two percent of their account on a single trade.

Position Sizing: Depending on your risk tolerance, position size determines how much money is allotted to each trade. The ideal trade size in relation to your account balance and stop-loss distance can be found with the aid of position sizing calculators. Levels of Stop-Loss and Take-Profit: While take-profit orders protect gains, stop-loss orders restrict losses. Consistent risk management is ensured by placing these levels intelligently, according to volatility or support and resistance.

Risk-Reward Ratio: A healthy risk-reward ratio, such as 1:2 or higher, suggests the possible return is at least twice the potential loss. This makes it possible to maintain profitability despite a decreased victory rate.

Preserving capital and avoiding rash decisions require effective risk management techniques.

Creating a Trading Plan.

A trading plan is the blueprint of your trading operations, covering every component of your strategy. Creating a thorough strategy will help you become more focused, disciplined, and consistent. Specify the requirements for entry and exit:

Indicate the circumstances in which you plan to enter and exit deals. This could entail employing chart patterns, indicators (such moving averages), or economic data releases as signals. Having clear criteria improves consistency and avoids emotional decision-making.

Establish Trade Timing Rules: Decide which timeframes to use for trading, such as the daily chart for swing trading or the 5-minute chart for scalping. Additionally, choose the trading hours according to the volatility of the selected currency pairings and your availability.

Create a Routine: You may stay organized and prepared by creating a daily routine that includes tasks like evaluating economic calendars, arranging transactions, and assessing market circumstances.

Performance Monitoring: Document every trade in your trading log, including entry and exit prices, position sizes, and outcomes. You may evaluate performance, spot trends, and improve your approach over time by going over previous trades.

Using Backtesting to Improve Your Approach Backtesting is the process of assessing a strategy's efficacy using past data. Before putting actual money at risk, traders can use this technique to determine their strengths and shortcomings.

Choosing Historical Data: To obtain a thorough understanding of the performance of your strategy, pick a time frame that encompasses a variety of market situations (such as trends and ranges). Applying the Strategy: Simulate transactions according to the guidelines of your strategy using software or manual techniques. To compute important metrics like win rate, average profit/loss, and drawdowns, keep track of each trade's result.

Analyzing Outcomes: Consider measures including the strategy's consistency, profitability, and risk-reward ratio.

Determine what has to be improved, such as the entrance criteria or stop-loss levels.

Paper Trading: To build confidence in real-world market conditions, think about rehearsing your approach in a demo account after backtesting. You can hone your strategy with paper trading without taking any financial risks. Paper trading and backtesting are important phases in creating a dependable, tried-and-true technique that works well in practical settings.

Modifying Your Approach Based on Market Situations

Since markets are always changing, adaptability is essential. Performance can be greatly impacted by your ability to modify your plan in response to market conditions.

Trending vs. Ranging Markets: Use indicators like the Average Directional Index (ADX) to assess whether the market is trending or ranging. For trending markets, use trend-following tactics; for sideways markets, use range trading. Adjustments for volatility: While low volatility permits tighter stops, high volatility necessitates wider stop-loss settings. Modify the risk management guidelines in your plan to reflect the volatility of the present.
News Events: Significant news events might interfere with regular

trading patterns, such as pronouncements from central banks or changes in the geopolitical landscape. To deal with rising volatility, think about halting trading or changing your approach.

Currency-Specific Factors: Certain currency pairs are more susceptible to particular economic variables or are more volatile than others. Adjust your approach based on the traits of the pairings you trade; for example, steer clear of particular pairs when there is less liquidity. Your plan will stay profitable and relevant in a variety of market scenarios if you are flexible.

Typical Strategy Errors to Avoid

Both novice and seasoned traders encounter typical hazards that can compromise the effectiveness of their strategies. Here are several errors to be aware of:

Overcomplicating the Strategy: Analytical paralysis can result from complex strategies that use an excessive number of indicators or criteria. Focus on high-probability setups and maintain a straightforward approach. Ignoring the Big Picture: Making bad decisions might result from concentrating just on short-term signals and ignoring broader patterns or underlying causes. **Too Many Strategy Changes**: Changing tactics too soon after a few setbacks keeps you from thoroughly assessing your strategy. Before making any adjustments, give your plan some time to work.

Absence of discipline: If not used consistently, even the best plan may backfire. Adhere to your principles and refrain from making snap judgments or decisions based on feelings.

By avoiding these typical blunders, strategy efficacy and long-term success can be increased.

Chapter 6

The Psychology of Forex Trading

Overview of the Psychology of Trading

The term "trading psychology" describes the mental and emotional aspects that affect a trader's choices. Trading presents a special psychological challenge since, in contrast to other occupations, it entails ongoing exposure to risk, uncertainty, and the possibility of financial gain or loss. By encouraging discipline, patience, and resilience, knowing and mastering trading psychology can greatly enhance your success. This chapter will look at major psychological pitfalls that traders encounter, the value of emotional regulation, and methods for developing a positive trading mindset.

Managing Emotions in Trading

In forex trading, where impatience, greed, and fear can result in bad choices, emotional management is crucial.

The main feelings that traders experience and their effects are as follows

Fear: The fear of losing money might cause people to hesitate or leave too soon, which can result in lost chances.

A string of losses frequently triggers fear, which makes traders unduly cautious or suspicious.

Greed: Greed can lead traders to disregard risk management guidelines or take needless risks. As traders try to maximize gains without taking the downside into account, this frequently results in overtrading, revenge trading, and excessive leverage.

Impatience: Impatience can result in rash actions, especially in markets that move quickly. In order to prevent profitable deals from realizing their full potential, traders may enter trades without conducting adequate analysis or quit too soon.

Overconfidence: Traders may become overconfident following a string of profitable deals, which could result in riskier transactions and a disrespect for their trading strategy. When the market turns, this frequently leads to large losses.

It is essential to acknowledge and control these feelings in order to continue dealing in a fair and impartial manner.

Typical Psychological Fallacies.
Thought patterns known as psychological traps might influence trading decisions negatively.

The following are some that traders commonly come across:

Loss Aversion: Loss aversion is the inclination to fear losses more than valuing similar benefits. This can result in closing winning deals too soon to "lock in" earnings or holding onto losing trades longer than required in the hopes that they would rebound. Recency bias is the tendency for traders to place greater emphasis on recent occurrences than on past patterns. For example, traders may get overconfident after a successful trade because they think similar settings will produce the same outcomes. Confirmation bias is the propensity to ignore contradicting facts in favor of information that supports one's ideas. This could lead traders to maintain a position in trading even when fresh information indicates that it should be sold.

The Sunk Cost Fallacy is a trap that traders fall into when they keep a bad deal going because they have already spent a lot of time or money on it. Instead of reducing their losses, they wait for a potential reversal. By identifying these psychological pitfalls, traders can improve their self-awareness and steer clear of actions that impair performance.

Developing a Winning Mentality

To succeed in forex over the long run, one must have a winning mindset. It encompasses traits like perseverance, dedication, and fortitude that support traders in sticking to their goals and adjusting to shifting market conditions. Here's how to cultivate these qualities: Regardless of the state of the market or your feelings, discipline entails sticking to your trading strategy. Routines, including performance evaluations and daily analysis, help you stay focused and encourage discipline. Waiting for the best trade opportunities and letting trades to their full potential need patience. Learning to wait can significantly increase profitability because impulsive trades frequently result in unfavorable consequences.

Resilience: Losses are unavoidable in trading. The capacity to recover from setbacks without losing hope is resilience. This entails accepting losses as a necessary component of learning and growing from errors.

Adaptability: Because the forex market is always shifting, traders must be able to adjust to new circumstances and trends. Remaining relevant in the industry requires being willing to learn new things and improve existing tactics.

By developing these traits, traders can stay composed and concentrated, which lowers the possibility of emotional trading.

Establishing a Journal for Personal Trading

One effective technique for monitoring and enhancing trading psychology is a trading journal. It enables traders to pinpoint areas in need of development by offering insight into decision-making procedures, emotional states, and performance trends.

Keeping Track of Trade Information: Keep track of each trade's entry and departure points, position size, motivations, and results. Before, during, and after every deal, make notes about your mental condition.

Monitoring Emotional Trends: To spot emotional trends, go over your journal on a regular basis. For instance, you might observe that overconfidence resulted in riskier bets or that fear made you abandon trades too soon. **Examining Errors and Gains**: Consider both profitable and unprofitable transactions. Taking into account both technical and psychological factors, determine what worked and what may have been improved.

Establishing Improvement Goals: Make use of the knowledge you gain from your journal to establish clear objectives. If impatience is a problem for you, for example, make it a goal to wait for confirmation before making transactions.

By encouraging self-awareness, a trading notebook enables traders to gradually enhance their approach and perspective.

Engaging in Stress Reduction and Mindfulness Because trading may be emotionally and cognitively taxing, stress management is essential for long-term success. Deep breathing and meditation are two mindfulness practices that can help traders focus better and reduce stress.

Mindfulness Meditation: By increasing self-awareness, meditation can assist traders in identifying and controlling their emotions when they surface. It has been demonstrated that regular mindfulness meditation improves decision-making and lowers stress.

Deep Breathing Exercises: By calming the mind, simple breathing techniques might help traders make more thoughtful decisions and less impulsive decisions.

Taking Breaks: Burnout can result from constant exposure to market data.

The mind can be rejuvenated and emotional exhaustion avoided by taking breaks in between trading sessions.

Physical Activity: Engaging in regular exercise helps traders perform better by lowering stress, enhancing focus, and fostering general well-being. By incorporating these techniques into your everyday routine, you can improve resilience and emotional control while decreasing the probability of making snap decisions based on feelings.

Establishing a Practice for Ongoing Enhancement

The process of improving trading mentality is continuous. Traders can maintain their focus on personal development and progress by establishing routines and goals.

Weekly Performance Review: Examine your transactions and trading log at the conclusion of each week to evaluate your performance, pinpoint errors, and recognize accomplishments. Pay attention to both the psychological and technical components.

Setting Monthly Objectives: Set monthly objectives to focus on particular areas that need work, including cutting back on overtrading, following your plan, or managing your greed and fear.

Learning from Other Traders: Reading books on trading psychology, participating in trading communities, and observing the strategies of profitable traders can all provide insightful information. Gaining knowledge from others can also inspire you and open your eyes.

Adapting as Necessary: To make sure your trading strategy and mentality remain in line with your objectives, periodically assess and improve your approach. You could discover that some routines or strategies require modification as you acquire experience. As long as traders continue to work on themselves, their psyche will remain as sharp as their technical and foundational abilities.

An overview of Chapter 6 The psychological components of forex trading were covered in Chapter 6, including developing a winning mindset, emotional management, and frequent psychological pitfalls. We talked about doable methods for practicing mindfulness, keeping a personal trading journal, controlling emotions, and developing a pattern for ongoing development. Long-term success requires resilience, discipline, and self-awareness, all of which traders can develop by studying trading psychology. We'll explore risk management fundamentals in the upcoming chapter, including strategies to protect capital and boost profitability.

Chapter 7

Risk Management Essentials

Overview of Risk Management

One of the most important parts of forex trading is risk control. Although strategy and analysis are crucial, risk management keeps losses under control and avoidable. Capital is safeguarded, regular trading is made possible, and long-term profitability is established through efficient risk management.

The fundamentals of risk management, including position size, take-profit and stop-loss orders, and risk-reward analysis, will be covered in this chapter.

The Value of Take-Profit and Stop-Loss Orders

Two essential instruments for controlling risk and ensuring profits are stop-loss and take-profit orders. Stop-Loss Order: A stop-loss order limits possible losses by setting a predetermined order to close a trade if it hits a specific level. below avoid further losses, for instance, if you purchase EUR/USD at 1.1200 and set a stop-loss at 1.1150, the trade would automatically shut if the price drops below 1.1150. Take-Profit Order: When a trade hits a predetermined profit threshold, a take-profit order ends the trade. For example, if you have a long EUR/USD trade with a take-profit set at 1.1250, the trade will automatically close when the price hits that level, protecting your earnings. By placing these orders, traders can minimize emotional involvement and handle trades without continual oversight.

The Risk-Reward Ratio Calculation

The potential profit of a trade in relation to its possible risk is measured by the risk-reward ratio. This ratio guarantees that rewards outweigh risks and assists traders in determining whether a trade is worthwhile.

The computation involves dividing the possible profit by the possible loss.

The risk-reward ratio is 1:2, for instance, if you risk 50 pip to make 100 pip. Optimal Ratios: To ensure that possible gains are double the potential loss, many traders strive for a minimum risk-reward ratio of 1:2. Additional profit potential is offered by ratios of 1:3 or greater, but the trade setup and technique should determine the ratio.

A good risk-reward ratio is crucial when making trading decisions because it enables traders to stay profitable even with a reduced success rate.

Calculating Lot Size and Position.

The amount of capital allotted to each trade is determined by position size, which takes into account the trader's account balance and risk tolerance. By keeping the possible loss on each transaction to a reasonable amount, proper position sizing protects capital during losing streaks.

Risk Per Trade:

Generally speaking, you should risk 1% to 2% of your account balance each trade. Your maximum permitted loss per trade, for instance, is $100 if you have a $10,000 account balance and you risk 1% on each trade.

Lot Size Calculation: The number of currency units in a trade is determined by the lot size. For instance, you can use a position sizing calculator to get the right lot size if you have a stop-loss of 50 pip and a maximum risk of $100. Maintaining losses within reasonable bounds and enabling traders to continue trading during drawdowns depend on efficient position sizing.

The Use of Trailing Stops

One kind of stop-loss that automatically modifies as the transaction advances in your favor is a trailing stop. By bringing the stop level closer to the present price, it locks in profits, permitting possible gains while guarding against reversals. In the event that the price increases in your favor, the stop-loss level will rise by 20 pips, for instance, if you have a trailing stop of 20 pips set.

The transaction will close and the profit will be locked in if the price then reverses by 20 pip. Benefits: By preventing reversals, trailing stops enable traders to profit from rising markets. For lengthier trades where price swings can be unpredictable, they are very helpful. Trailing stops offer a compromise between protecting profits and letting transactions execute to their maximum potential.

Risk Diversification

Instead of focusing on a single trade or market, diversification entails distributing risk among several currency pairs or assets.

By lowering exposure to any one trade, this strategy aids in return stabilization.

Trading Multiple pairings: Traders can spread their cash over a number of currency pairings rather than risking a sizable amount on a single trade. For instance, a trader could divide their investment among EUR/USD, GBP/USD, and USD/JPY rather than making a large investment in EUR/USD.

Non-Correlated Pairs: To increase variety, pick currency pairs that don't move in lockstep. If you're long USD/JPY, for example, you could want to short a separate pair that has little to do with USD/JPY. By lessening the influence of any one trade or market swing, traders can attain a more consistent performance through risk diversification.

Restricting the Use of Leverage

Excessive leverage can increase losses just as much as it can increase gains, even if it enables traders to manage huge positions with little cash. It is crucial to properly manage leverage in order to avoid suffering large losses. Selecting the Right Leverage Level: A leverage ratio of 1:10 or less is preferred by many traders. Although greater leverage, such as 1:100, might boost possible profits, it also raises risk and makes it more difficult to recover from losses.

Avoiding Over-Leverage: One of the primary causes of traders' significant losses is over-leveraging. Traders can lower the danger of leverage by trading smaller positions in relation to the size of their accounts. When traders use leverage properly, they can seize chances without risking losing all of their money.

Establishing Weekly and Daily Loss Caps Traders are prevented from overtrading or taking unwarranted risks during losing streaks by daily and weekly loss limitations.

Establishing these boundaries is a proactive approach to capital preservation and mental equilibrium.

The highest amount a trader is willing to lose in a single day is known as the daily loss limit.

The trader should cease trading for the remainder of the day after reaching this point.

A lot of traders put this limit between two and three percent of their account balance.

Weekly Loss Limit:

The weekly limit is the highest allowable loss for a trading week, much like the daily limit. Traders can use this limit to reset, evaluate their performance, and modify their strategy for the upcoming week. Setting loss limits helps traders avoid chasing losses, which lowers the likelihood that they would make rash decisions during drawdowns.

The Value of a Risk Management Strategy
A thorough manual for controlling risk in all trades is called a risk management plan. It assists traders in staying consistent, refraining from snap judgments, and achieving sustained financial success.

A risk management plan's components should include standards for risk-reward ratios, maximum drawdown limits, risk per trade, and regulations for leverage and diversification.

Consistency: Adhering to a clear risk management strategy guarantees that every trade is handled with the same level of discipline, which lessens emotional reactions to specific gains or losses.

An organized approach to trading is offered by a well-written risk management plan, which improves consistency and resilience in the face of market swings.

Assessing and Improving Your Approach to Risk Management.

Risk management is dynamic and should be reviewed and modified on a regular basis to accommodate shifting market conditions and individual trading development. **Frequent Review**: Every month or every three months, evaluate your risk management procedures. Examine whether your position sizes match your risk tolerance, whether your loss limits have stopped excessive losses, and whether your risk-reward ratio is sustainable. Adapting to Market Conditions: Take into account lowering leverage or modifying stop-loss levels during times of high volatility.

On the other hand, you could raise the amount of your stake within safe bounds in markets that are stable. **Learning from Mistakes**: Take advantage of all setbacks as teaching moments.

Determine the trends that resulted in significant losses and think about making changes to avoid recurring circumstances.

Frequent review guarantees that risk management procedures continue to be efficient and in line with your changing trading style as well as market conditions.

An overview of Chapter. 7

The fundamentals of risk management in forex trading were

discussed in Chapter 7. This chapter emphasized the instruments and procedures that safeguard capital and guarantee steady growth, from establishing stop-loss and take-profit orders to computing risk-reward ratios and employing position sizing efficiently.

Even in difficult market situations, traders can develop resilience and keep control by limiting leverage, diversifying risk, and establishing daily and weekly loss limits. We will examine the resources and tools that facilitate successful forex trading as we proceed to Chapter 8, assisting traders in remaining knowledgeable and prepared for success.

Chapter 8

Forex Trading Tools and Resources

Overview of Forex Trading Instruments.

To properly assess, execute, and monitor trades, forex trading necessitates the use of the appropriate tools and resources in addition to a plan and discipline. With the correct configuration, traders can acquire market data, make decisions more quickly, and improve their tactics. We'll go over important tools and resources in this chapter, including as news sources, trading platforms, charting software, and economic calendars.

Marketplaces for Trading

You can conduct transactions, examine charts, and keep an eye on your portfolio using a trading platform. It serves as the principal contact between the trader and the forex market. Well-known trading systems consist of: MetaTrader 4 (MT4): MT4 is well-known for its broad feature set and easy-to-use interface. It provides technical indicators, sophisticated charting tools, and automated trading via Expert Advisors (EAs). It offers a strong trading experience and is quite well-liked by FX traders. More timeframes, economic calendars, and a wider variety of order types are among the features that MetaTrader 5 (MT5), the replacement for MT4, offers. It is appropriate for traders who require access to other asset classes and a little more freedom. cTrader: Traders that value speed and transparency prefer cTrader, a robust platform with sophisticated charting and order execution features. It is renowned for its high degree of customization and user-friendly interface. TradingView: TradingView is a web-based application that provides social networking capabilities together with robust graphing tools. TradingView integration is supported by several brokers, albeit not all of them have direct connections. For traders seeking a cooperative setting, its extensive array of indicators and social elements are perfect. The amount of tools needed, broker compatibility, and personal preferences all play a role in selecting the best platform.

Software for Charting.

With the use of charting software, traders may see price data, spot trends, and use indicators to carry out technical analysis. Although many trading platforms come with built-in charting capabilities, more sophisticated tools are frequently available through standalone charting software: MetaTrader (MT4/MT5): Both MT4 and MT5 include a wide range of charting features, including as different timeframes, customisable indicators, and chart templates.

TradingView: With thousands of customisable indicators, drawing tools, and the ability to write custom scripts using Pine Script (TradingView's scripting language), TradingView offers a wide range of charting features.

Its collaborative capabilities and simple UI make it very popular.

NinjaTrader: Well-liked by professional traders, NinjaTrader is renowned for its sophisticated charting and analytics features. It is typically utilized for stocks and futures, but it also supports real-time market data, backtesting, and custom indicators.

Traders can study historical data, spot trends, and make data-driven trading decisions with the aid of effective charting tools.

Calendars of Economic Events
Future data releases and economic events that could affect the currency market are listed on an economic calendar.

Key events include GDP statistics, inflation rates, job data, and central bank announcements.

Planning trades and controlling volatility require keeping abreast of these developments.

Forex Factory: With real-time updates and comprehensive details on every event, including its possible effects on currency pairs, Forex Factory's economic calendar is popular.

Investing.com: Traders can concentrate on the events that are most pertinent to their trading strategy with the help of Investing.com's economic calendar, which offers an intuitive interface with adjustable filters.

Myfxbook: This resource is useful for fundamental analysis since it provides an economic calendar together with extra capabilities like sentiment analysis and historical event analysis.

By keeping traders updated on high-impact events, an economic calendar lowers the chance that they will be caught off guard by news that could move the market.

Sources of News and Analysis

For forex traders, having access to trustworthy, current news and analysis is essential.

Global events have a big influence on the currency market, and trading decisions can be greatly impacted by timely information.

<u>Reliable news and analysis sources include:</u>

Bloomberg: Bloomberg covers international markets and FX events and offers up-to-date financial news, economic statistics, and professional analysis.

It is renowned for both its coverage scope and accuracy.

Reuters: Another excellent news source, Reuters focuses on significant events that impact the foreign exchange market, such as shifts in economic policy and geopolitical developments.

DailyFX: This website provides news, analysis, and educational materials tailored to the currency market.

Traders looking for in-depth forex insights, such as technical and fundamental analysis, will find it very helpful.

FXStreet: FXStreet is a specialized forex news website that offers currency forecasts, economic updates, and technical analysis. Expert articles and sentiment indicators are also included.

Having trustworthy news sources guarantees that traders are informed about world events that may impact currency fluctuations and market volatility.

Calculators for Trading

Before making trades, trading calculators are useful for figuring out risk, margin, and possible profit or loss.

Typical kinds include

Position Size Calculator: Determines the ideal position size by taking into account the stop-loss distance, risk percentage, and account balance. For consistent risk management across trades, this tool is crucial.

A currency pair's pip value is determined by a pip calculator, which enables traders to evaluate the dollar amount at risk for each pip fluctuation.

The margin needed to open a trade is determined by the margin calculator, which takes into account the position size, currency pair, and leverage.

Profit/Loss Calculator:

Determines a trade's possible profit or loss based on position size and entry and exit prices. With the aid of trading calculators, traders may plan their deals and make sure that each one complies with their risk management policies.

Indicators of Sentiment

Sentiment indicators reveal whether the bulk of traders are long or short a currency pair by displaying the combined actions of other market participants.

Understanding the psychology of the market and possible reversals can be aided by this information. **Myfxbook Sentiment:**

The sentiment feature on Myfxbook displays the proportion of traders who are long or short major currency pairings.

Extremes of high sentiment (such as 90% long) may indicate a possible reversal.

OANDA Sentiment:

OANDA provides its customers with a sentiment indicator that shows the proportion of traders with long or short positions. It serves as a helpful indicator of market sentiment.

IG Client Sentiment:

Data from traders is displayed via IG's client sentiment tool, which indicates how many traders are long or short on certain pairs.

When sentiment reaches severe levels, it may signal future market turning moments.

When market sentiment is excessively bullish or pessimistic, sentiment indicators can shed light on possible reversals.

Tools for Backtesting

Before implementing their tactics in real-time markets, traders can test them on historical data using backtesting tools to assess their performance.

Backtesting aids in strategy refinement, boosting dependability and confidence.

MetaTrader Strategy Tester:

MT4 and MT5 come with an integrated strategy tester that lets traders test automated strategies and Expert Advisors (EAs) on historical data. TradingView Pine Script: This tool lets traders design and test their own indicators and strategies.
For anyone who wishes to develop and test their own strategies, it's a useful tool.
NinjaTrader: NinjaTrader provides sophisticated backtesting capabilities, such as comprehensive performance

metrics and optimization tools. Professional traders creating intricate techniques will find it ideal.

Before going live, traders can use backtesting tools to analyze possible performance, validate tactics, and make any necessary adjustments.

Learning Materials In Forex trading. Learning new things constantly is essential. Educational resources can help you increase your knowledge and sharpen your skills as a trader, regardless of your level of experience.

Babypips: Babypips provides a thorough "School of Pipsology," covering everything from fundamentals to sophisticated tactics in forex.

It's a popular resource for beginners and advanced traders.

Trading Books: Books like John Murphy's *"Technical Analysis of the Financial Markets"* and Dr. Alexander Elder's *"Trading for a Living"* offer comprehensive information and insights on forex trading strategies.

 Free webinars, live trading sessions, and online courses covering trading methods, technical analysis, and market insights are provided by a number of brokers and platforms, including DailyFX and FXStreet.

Trading Communities: Participating in social media groups, online forums, or trading communities—like those on Facebook or Reddit—can yield helpful advice and assistance. Talking with other traders keeps merchants engaged and promotes learning.

Trading professionals can improve their expertise, hone their tactics, and keep up with market developments with the aid of educational tools.

An overview of Chapter 8 The key resources and technologies that facilitate forex trading were examined in Chapter 8. Every instrument, from trading platforms and charting software to economic calendars and educational materials, contributes to improving strategy creation, risk management, and decision-making. With these tools at their disposal, traders may approach the market more accurately and confidently. We will go over starting tactics in the upcoming chapter, taking novice traders step-by-step through the fundamentals of making trades and avoiding typical traps.

Chapter 9

Forex for Beginners – A Step-by-Step Guide

An Overview of Forex Trading for Novices Because of the language, platforms, and tactics involved, it might be intimidating for a novice to enter the forex market. Nonetheless, a methodical approach can boost confidence and streamline the learning process. From comprehending currency pairs to placing your first trade, this chapter offers a comprehensive how-to for novices.

New traders can lay a strong basis for a profitable forex experience by following these steps.

Selecting an Account and Selecting a Broker.

Choosing a broker and opening an account is the first step in your journey. The forex market, trading platforms, and learning aids are all accessible through the appropriate broker.

Investigate Brokers.

Pick a trustworthy broker who is subject to financial authorities' regulations. Check for things like customer service, available currency pairs, transaction costs, and leverage choices.

Create a Demo Account:

The majority of brokers let you practice trading with virtual money by offering demo accounts. To master platform navigation and testing techniques, a sample account is a great resource.

Fund Your Account: To reduce risk, make a small initial deposit when you're ready to start a live account. Because forex trading is risky, start with money you are willing to lose. The first step in using the forex market is creating an account, and using a trial account to practice might help you become more confident.

Knowledge of Currency Pairs and Their Trading Techniques.

Currency pairs are bought and sold in forex trading, where the base currency is one and the quote currency is the other. Learn about the operation of currency pairs:

Major Pairs: These are USD-related pairs, such as EUR/USD and USD/JPY. Because major pairs are stable, they are quite liquid and appropriate for novices.

Every currency pair has a bid price, which is the price at which you may sell, and an ask price, which is the price at which you can purchase.

The spread, or the cost of the trade, is what separates these.

Calculating Pip Value: Determining profit or loss is made easier with an understanding of pip value. For instance, one pip change in EUR/USD is equivalent to $10 in a typical lot (100,000 units). Gaining an understanding of these fundamentals will enable novices to effectively assess currency pair pricing and understand how the forex market functions.

Using a Demo Account to Practice

Use a demo account to practice trading before going live.

This enables you to test tactics, become acquainted with the trading platform, and comprehend market movements without having to risk real money.

Conduct Test Trades: Put buy and sell orders to examine how trades are carried out, become acquainted with the different kinds of orders, and watch how trades are opened and closed.

Test Take-Profit and Stop-Loss Orders:
To protect gains and control possible losses, practice placing take-profit and stop-loss orders. **Track Trades**: Track trades to learn how currency pairs react to technical levels, market circumstances, and economic events.

When switching to live trading, using a demo account lowers the learning curve and increases confidence.

An Introduction to Basic Technical Analysis.
Price charts and indicators are used in technical analysis to spot trends and forecast future moves.

In order to analyze market movements and make wise trading

decisions, beginners might begin with simple tools.

Candlestick Charts: These charts demonstrate how prices have changed over time, including the opening, closing, high, and low prices.

To spot possible reversals or continuations, learn to spot basic patterns like dojis and engulfing candles.

The price levels at which the currency pair has historically reversed or stalled are known as support and resistance levels. Whereas resistance is a level where selling pressure stops further increase, support is a level where purchasing interest is strong enough to stop further decline.

Moving Averages (MA): Moving averages highlight trends by smoothing out price data. Popular options for assisting novices in determining whether the market is in an uptrend or decline are the 50-day and 200-day moving averages. Beginners can analyze price movements and decide when to enter and exit markets with the help of basic technical analysis.

Beginning to Use Fundamental Analysis.

Fundamental analysis looks at news, geopolitical developments, and economic facts that affect currency values.

The first step for novices should be to comprehend important economic indicators: Interest rates are a tool used by central banks, such as the European Central Bank and the Federal Reserve, to regulate inflation and economic growth.

Because they draw in foreign investment, higher interest rates frequently make a currency stronger. GDP growth rates are a measure of the state of the economy. A rising GDP makes a currency stronger, whilst a falling GDP can make it weaker. Employment Information: Stability in the economy is reflected in employment rates.

For instance, increasing consumer spending and economic stability brought about by lower unemployment can make a currency stronger.

Understanding the influence of basic variables on currency fluctuations is made easier for novices by keeping up with economic releases and news.

Your First Purchase.

The next step is to execute a live trade after you are at ease with demo trading. Follow these steps to make your first trade: Select a Currency Pair: Choose a pair that you are familiar with, preferably one that has less volatility at first, like EUR/USD.

Examine the Market:

To determine whether to purchase or sell, use fundamental or basic technical analysis.

Establish the Take-Profit, Stop-Loss, and Entry Levels.

To reduce possible losses, decide where to enter the trade and establish a stop-loss level.

Establish a take-profit threshold to protect profits in the event that the trade goes your way. Place the Trade: Make the trade using the interface provided by your broker. Keep an eye on it to observe how price fluctuations match your findings. Although it can be frightening, making your first transaction is a crucial learning experience for moving from theory to practice.

Preventing Typical Beginner

A lot of novices make mistakes that can cost them money.

You can increase your chances of success by identifying and avoiding these errors:

Over-leveraging: Excessive leverage increases the possibility of losses. Leverage should be kept to a minimum for beginners until they gain experience and confidence. **Ignoring Stop-Loss Orders**: Trades are susceptible to unanticipated reversals when stop-loss orders are not set. To control risk, always place stop-loss orders.

Overtrading: Putting in too many deals, usually out of excitement or impatience, raises the risk and expense of transactions. Prioritize quality over quantity and start with fewer trades.

Emotional Trading: Impulsive decisions might result from fear, greed, and impatience.

When making decisions, follow your trading plan and avoid letting your emotions guide you.

Beginners can safeguard their wealth and maintain their focus on long-term success by avoiding these typical blunders.

Creating a Basic Trading Strategy

A trading plan helps you maintain discipline and gives you structure. A basic strategy can have a significant impact on maintaining consistency and attention.

Establish Your Objectives: Establish attainable objectives, such learning to recognize good setups or increasing a specific percentage of return per month. Select a Plan: Choose a trading approach that works for you, such swing or day trading. Adhere to this plan and refrain from trying out different strategies.

Establish Risk Parameters: Use position sizing to keep your risk tolerance within the parameters you have established for each trade.

Review and Improve: Keep a log of your trades, noting what worked and what needs work.

Over time, adjust your strategy in light of these revelations.

Beginners can maintain discipline, attention, and a grounded attitude to trading with the aid of a basic trading plan.

Putting Discipline and Patience into Practice

It takes discipline and patience to trade forex, especially when you're first starting out. Don't rush the learning process and keep in mind that steady improvement is more important than rapid financial gain.

Hold Off for Quality Setups:

Waiting for a high-probability trade situation is preferable to making transactions on the spur of the moment.

Accept Losses as a Part of the Process: Learning is a process that will inevitably involve losses. Consistency is more important than winning every trade.

Adhere to Your Plan.

Making rash decisions is less likely when you stick to your trading plan. Recall that a crucial characteristic of profitable traders is discipline. Beginners can cultivate the attitude required for sustained success in forex trading by exercising patience and discipline.

An overview of Chapter 9 For those new to the currency market, Chapter 9 offered a detailed guide. This chapter highlights a methodical approach to learning forex trading, covering everything from selecting a broker and practicing on a demo account to placing your first transaction and avoiding typical errors. New traders can lay a strong basis for long-term success with patience, discipline, and a straightforward trading strategy. We will examine more complex trading methods in Chapter 10, giving traders the tools and tactics they need to develop their abilities.

Chapter 10

Advanced Forex Trading Techniques

Overview of Sophisticated Trading Methods

As traders gain experience, they generally seek additional ways to better their performance and exploit more sophisticated trading chances. By using sophisticated analysis, indicators, and occasionally automation, advanced strategies enable traders to take use of tools and insights that can increase profitability. Advanced techniques like utilizing indicators and oscillators, comprehending chart patterns, implementing risk management modifications, and investigating algorithmic trading will all be covered in this chapter.

Making Use of Oscillators and Technical Indicators.

Traders can examine price trends, momentum, and possible reversals with the aid of technical indicators and oscillators.

To improve entry and exit signals, experienced traders frequently mix many indicators.

Moving Average Convergence Divergence (MACD)

This trend-following indicator illustrates how two moving averages relate to one another. Opportunities to purchase or sell may be indicated by the MACD line crossing above or below the signal line. On a scale of 0 to 100, the Relative Strength Index (RSI) calculates the rate and direction of price changes. An overbought situation is usually indicated by an RSI above 70, whilst an oversold situation is suggested by an RSI below 30.

Bollinger Bands.

Two standard deviation lines above and below a center moving average line make up a Bollinger Band.

High volatility and possible reversals are frequently indicated when the price goes close to the bands.

Fibonacci Retracements.

Fibonacci retracement levels are useful for locating possible locations of resistance and support.

These levels—23.6%, 38.2%, 50%, and 61.8%—are used by traders to forecast when a market may retrace. By validating trends and determining the best times to enter and exit the market, the combination of oscillators and indicators helps improve decision-making.

Understanding Patterns in Charts
Expert traders forecast future price movements by analyzing chart patterns. Identifying trends and knowing how to respond to them can give you a big advantage.

Head and Shoulders: This three-peak pattern, with the middle peak being the highest, indicates a trend reversal. A bearish reversal is confirmed by a breakdown below the neckline.

Double Top and Double Bottom: While double bottoms imply bullish reversals, double tops indicate possible bearish ones. When the price doesn't break through a resistance or support level twice, these patterns are formed. Symmetrical, ascending, and descending triangles: These patterns frequently signify continuation, with prices first consolidating inside convergent trend lines then bursting out in the trend's direction. Short consolidations inside a strong trend are represented by flags and pennants, which, once broken, usually indicate continuance in the trend's direction. Gaining an understanding of chart patterns enables traders to capitalize on trend continuations and reversals and make timely decisions.

Advanced Methods of Risk Management.

In order to optimize gains while lowering risk, advanced traders frequently employ additional dynamic risk management techniques in addition to the conventional stop-loss and take-profit orders.

Closing a portion of a position when the trade hits a specific profit threshold is known as partial profit-taking. With this strategy, some earnings are locked in while the remaining half is left open for future profit potential.

Trailing Stops with Custom Intervals: Advanced traders can modify the stop loss in response to recent volatility or price action rather than employing a fixed trailing stop. To provide more flexibility during turbulent times, they might, for example, trail a stop based on ATR (Average True Range).

Hedging.

To lower risk exposure, hedging is initiating a position in the opposite direction of an active trade.

To counteract possible losses, a trader who is long EUR/USD but expects short-term volatility can open a short position on a connected pair, such as GBP/USD. More control over capital is possible with advanced risk management strategies that balance profit potential with risk exposure.

Examining Automated and Algorithmic.

Algorithmic trading, sometimes known as "algo trading," is the practice of executing trades according to preset criteria using automated systems.

Efficiency, stability, and a less emotional investment in trading are all benefits of automation. Automated trading algorithms known as Expert Advisors (EAs) are accessible on platforms such as MT4 and MT5. EAs can handle transactions based on technical indicators, chart patterns, or other rules when traders specify certain requirements for trade execution.

High-Frequency Trading (HFT): This type of algorithmic trading involves programs that make hundreds of deals every second in an attempt to profit from little fluctuations in price.

HFT is usually utilized by big financial institutions rather than individual traders and necessitates a substantial amount of processing capacity.

Backtesting and Optimization: To ascertain possible profitability, experienced traders test algorithms on past data.

By examining performance across a range of market scenarios, backtesting enables traders to improve their algorithms.

 The use of a virtual private server, or VPS, guarantees that automated strategies continue to function uninterrupted even when the trader's computer is turned off.

For traders who depend on round-the-clock automation, this is essential.

Although algorithmic trading can boost productivity, its effectiveness depends on thorough testing, optimization, and oversight.

Comprehending Diversification and Correlation.

In order to comprehend how various currency pairs move in respect to one another, advanced traders frequently research the correlation between them.

Overall risk is decreased by diversifying across non-correlated couples. Positive currency pairs, such as EUR/USD and GBP/USD, tend to move in tandem, whereas negative currency pairs, such as EUR/USD and USD/JPY, move in opposition to one another.

Hedging Using Correlated Pairs:
To protect their trades, some traders employ correlated pairs.
 For instance, if a trader expects risk in the USD, a long position in EUR/USD may be hedged by a short position in USD/JPY.
Diversifying Across Asset Classes: In order to expose themselves to a variety of market circumstances, advanced traders might diversify their holdings beyond forex by trading

commodities, indices, or cryptocurrencies.

By lowering dependence on any one currency or market scenario, diversification and an understanding of correlation aid in risk management.

Trading When News Events Have a Big Impact.

Significant volatility is produced by high-impact news items like employment reports, central bank statements, and geopolitical developments.

By using specific techniques, experienced traders can profit from these changes.

News Trading Strategy: News traders take advantage of abrupt market fluctuations by placing transactions as soon as significant news releases occur.

In order to profit from volatility, they prioritize speed and liquidity, frequently closing trades in a matter of minutes.

Before a significant news event, a straddle strategy is putting buy and sell orders on either side of the current price.

One of the orders is activated to record the movement if the price breaks out in either direction.

Risk Management in Volatile Markets:

In order to account for heightened volatility, advanced traders modify risk parameters during news events by lowering position sizes and extending stop-loss levels.

Rapid responses, in-depth market knowledge, and stringent risk management are necessary when trading during high-impact events.

Creating an Approach to Multi-Timeframe.

Multi-timeframe analysis is the process of examining various timeframes (such as five minutes, an hour, or a day) in order to validate patterns and enhance the precision of trading signals.

Top-Down Analysis: To find entry and exit points within a trend, start with longer timeframes (daily or weekly, for example) and work your way down to shorter ones (one hour or fifteen minutes).

Consistency Across Timeframes: It boosts confidence to validate trading signals across several timeframes. For instance, a purchase setup on the 1-hour chart is more dependable if the daily and 4-hour charts both display a positive trend.

A more comprehensive viewpoint is offered by multi-timeframe analysis, which aids traders in making more precise and knowledgeable trading selections.

Integrating Technical and Fundamental Analysis.

Although many traders concentrate on either technical or fundamental analysis, a more complete picture of the market can be obtained by combining the two.

Fundamental Analysis for Direction: To evaluate the general direction and sentiment of the market, use fundamental data, such as economic growth rates or central bank policies. For example, a trader would prefer deals that correspond with the strength of the USD if economic data points to a strong USD.

Technical Analysis for Timing: In the framework of the fundamental view, technical indications aid in the refinement of entry and exit locations. A trader who anticipates that EUR/USD would rise, for instance, might hold off on buying until they get an RSI oversold signal. By combining these strategies, traders are less likely to be influenced by technical indications or fundamentals without context, which helps them validate trade ideas.

Ongoing Education and Strategy Improvement.

The secret to expert trading is constant improvement. Profitable traders continuously evaluate their tactics, look for fresh perspectives, and adjust to shifting market conditions.

Maintaining a Trading Journal: Monitor transactions, tactics, and observations to pinpoint areas in need of development.

Keep track of how various circumstances impact performance and search for trends in both profitable and losing bets.

Acquiring New Skills: Keep up with market developments and new trading strategies, such as algorithmic breakthroughs or new economic regulations.

Your abilities remain competitive and relevant as a result. Adjusting to

Market Conditions: Since market conditions change over time, tactics that are effective now might not be tomorrow.

Continually improve tactics by adding fresh information and insights to make sure they continue to work.

Traders are kept ready for shifting markets and fresh trading chances by constant learning and adaptability.

An overview of Chapter 10 Advanced trading strategies were covered in Chapter 10, giving seasoned traders better instruments for managing, executing, and evaluating deals. These strategies improve trading accuracy and efficiency, ranging from using technical indicators and chart patterns to applying algorithmic trading and multi-timeframe analysis. Traders can maintain an advantage in the constantly changing foreign exchange market by adopting the proper strategies for risk management, diversification, and ongoing education. We'll look at case studies and actual situations in the upcoming chapter that demonstrate how the ideas and tactics discussed in this book can be used in real-world situations.

Chapter 11

Case Studies and Real-Life Examples

Overview of Case Studies in Forex
By demonstrating how trading strategies, analysis methodologies, and risk management measures are used in real-world situations, case studies provide priceless insights. We'll look at actual successful trade instances, typical errors, and lessons learnt in this chapter.

Traders can learn more about how theory works in practice, how to adjust to changing market conditions, and how to improve their own trading strategies by looking at these instances.

Use of Technical Analysis in a Trend-Following Approach.
Case Study 1

Background: A trader chose to use technical indicators as part of a trend-following strategy after seeing a significant rising trend in the EUR/USD pair.

Setup: To validate the trend, the trader employed the 50- and 200-day moving averages. The trader considered the 50-day moving average to be a strong buy signal if it passed over the 200-day (golden cross).

Execution: To lock in profits as the trend persisted, the trader started a buy position on EUR/USD and put a stop-loss just below the most recent swing bottom.

The 200-day moving average was used as a trailing stop.

Result: The trader's trailing stop enabled them to realize sizable gains as EUR/USD continued to increase.

The trailing stop was eventually activated by a bearish reversal, locking in winnings and closing the trade before the trend had turned around.

Lesson Learned: A trailing stop and moving averages worked well for riding the trend while controlling risk.

This case study emphasizes how crucial it is to use dynamic stop-losses in conjunction with trend-confirming indicators.

Case Study 2: Managing Risk in Situations of High Volatility
Background: A trader expected increased volatility during a U.S. Federal Reserve statement and chose to implement more stringent risk management procedures.

Setup: Although the trader was aware of the dangers of trading during high-impact news, they still wished to profit from any USD swings.

To limit possible losses, they cut their typical position size in half and set a stop-loss farther than usual, at a location that would permit more volatility.

Execution: Short before the news, the trader started a short position on GBP/USD. The currency pair had substantial price fluctuations as the news broke, but the bigger stop-loss kept the transaction from being closed too soon.

Result: The trader was able to achieve a minor profit after the GBP/USD exchange rate swung in their favor following an early rise. Wider stop-loss and smaller position size decreased risk exposure and avoided needless losses from early volatility.

Lesson Learned.

Risks can be controlled during volatile events by modifying stop-losses and position sizes in accordance with market conditions.

CASE STUDY 3

Technical Entry and Fundamentals-Driven

Trading Background: A trader noted that central bank policies and economic data supported a strong USD relative to the JPY, suggesting a long-term pessimistic view for the USD/JPY.

Setup: Based on a solid fundamental analysis, the trader chose to short the USD/JPY but awaited a technical entry.

On the daily chart, they saw a descending triangle, and the support level could be a breakout point.
Execution: The trader started a short position and set a stop-loss above the breakout level when the USD/JPY fell below the support level. They planned exit positions by using Fibonacci levels as take-profit targets.

Result: The USD/JPY kept falling until it hit the trader's Fibonacci take-profit levels.

As the trade developed, the trader reduced risk and secured profits by progressively exiting the trade at each level.

Lesson Learned: When technical patterns support the overall market perspective, combining technical entry points with fundamental analysis can improve trade accuracy.

Case Study 4:

Steer clear of emotional decision-making when you're losing money on a trade Background:

The trade began to move against a trader who had a long position on EUR/GBP.

The trader was tempted to hang with the deal in the hopes of a turnaround as losses increased.

Setup: The trader's emotions caused them to forgo establishing a stop-loss, despite their original plan. Rather, they continued to lower their stop-loss in the hopes that the market would finally turn around. **Execution**:

A considerable drop resulted from the trader holding the position while EUR/GBP kept falling.

The trade was eventually closed after they suffered a significant loss. **Result**: The trader's confidence and overall account balance were affected by the larger-than-expected loss that came from their emotional decision to hang onto the lost deal. **Lesson Learned**: Discipline issues and emotional decision-making can result in large losses. This example highlights how crucial it is to establish and follow stop-losses in order to prevent a minor loss from becoming a significant one.

Case Study 5.

Boot Effective Scalping Technique in a Market with Range Limitations

Background: A trader saw that the USD/CHF market was range-bound, alternating between levels of support and resistance.

Setup: The trader employed a scalping method, placing tight stop-losses on each trade and placing purchase orders at support and sell levels, respectively.

Execution: The trader established a tiny position with the goal of making rapid, moderate profit whenever USD/CHF approached the support or resistance level.

They kept a close eye on price movement and immediately closed trades when the price moved in their favor.

Result: The trader made modest but steady gains in the range-bound market by adhering to their scalping method.

In order to avoid losses from possible breakouts, they left the deal as volatility rose.

Lesson Learned: A scalping technique with tight stop-losses might work well in markets that are range-bound.

The need of adjusting tactics to the state of the market and knowing when to leave the range is illustrated by this example.

Case Study 6:

Applying Back Tested Strategies to Algorithmic Trading Background: Using technical indicators such as the RSI and MACD, an experienced trader developed an algorithm to automate a breakout strategy. Setup: To guarantee peak performance, the trader created and back tested the algorithm using historical data.

They evaluated the algorithm's performance in a variety of market scenarios, utilizing both trend and range markets.

Execution: The trader implemented the algorithm on a live account following a successful backtest.

The algorithm, which ran continually on a VPS, entered and exited transactions automatically when certain circumstances were met. **Result**: The algorithm executed transactions with discipline and accuracy, producing steady returns. To keep up with changes in the market, the trader examined and modified the algorithm on a regular basis.

Lesson Learned: Although algorithmic trading necessitates extensive testing and upkeep, it can increase efficiency and lessen emotional bias. Prior to live deployment, backtesting is crucial for determining strengths and flaws.

Case Study 7
Using Unrelated Currency Pairs to Diversify Background: By

diversifying across non-correlated currency pairs, with a particular emphasis on EUR/USD and USD/JPY, a trader aimed to lower risk.

Setup: By using correlation research, the trader discovered that the euro and yen were influenced by distinct variables, which frequently caused EUR/USD and USD/JPY to move independently. In the hope that diversification would lessen the impact of unforeseen market swings, they invested the same amount of money in each trade.

Execution: By holding long positions in EUR/USD and short positions in USD/JPY, the trader was able to profit from the separate price movements of each transaction. They kept a careful eye on both pairs and modified the stop-loss thresholds in response to each pair's performance.

Result: Each pair responded differently to USD volatility, with EUR/USD increasing and USD/JPY staying steady.

By reducing drawdowns, the trader's diversification technique produced a balanced portfolio performance.

Lesson Learned: Spreading investments among uncorrelated currency pairings lowers the influence of volatility on overall performance and aids in risk management.

Important Lessons Learned from Case Studies.

This chapter's case studies highlight a number of crucial ideas:

1. **Adapting to Market Conditions**: Whether the market is trending, range, or volatile, successful traders modify their techniques to fit the circumstances.

2. **Combining Analysis Methods**: Trade decisions can be strengthened and accuracy increased by utilizing both technical and fundamental analysis.

3. **Developing Emotional Discipline:** Maintaining emotional control is crucial to avoiding expensive errors, particularly when trading losing positions.

4. **Using Technology**: Algorithmic trading can increase productivity, but its effective application depends on optimization and backtesting.

5. **Diversification for Risk Management:**

By spreading investments across unrelated methods or pairs, you can lower overall risk and steady returns.

An overview of Chapter 11

Real-world examples and case studies that highlight important trading ideas, tactics, and lessons from both profitable and bad trades are presented in Chapter 11. Traders can gain a better understanding of how to put theory into practice, adjust to changing market conditions, and cultivate a more resilient and disciplined approach by studying these scenarios. Future trends in forex trading will be discussed in the upcoming chapter, along with new tools, possibilities, and technology that could influence the industry going forward.

Chapter 12.

Future Trends in Forex Trading

Overview of New Developments in Forex Changes in global economies, technological breakthroughs, and regulatory frameworks all have an impact on the currency market's constant evolution.

Traders may stay ahead of the curve, modify their tactics, and seize fresh chances by keeping an eye on rising trends.

Potential future developments in forex trading are examined in this chapter, including the impact of cryptocurrencies, the rise of artificial intelligence, the rise in algorithmic trading, and changes in regulatory procedures.

Machine Learning and Artificial Intelligence in Forex.

By offering strong instruments for data analysis, predictive modeling, and automation, artificial intelligence (AI) and machine learning (ML) are revolutionizing forex trading.

Algorithm Optimization: By examining enormous datasets and spotting trends that people would miss, AI can improve trading algorithms. As fresh data is processed, machine learning algorithms can adjust over time to increase accuracy.

Sentiment Analysis: To determine the mood of the market, AI can examine news stories, social media messages, and other textual sources. This can assist traders predict trends and changes in mood by offering insights into market psychology.

Automated Pattern Recognition: By training machine learning models to automatically identify technical patterns in price charts, technical analysis can become more effective and decision-making can happen more quickly.

Retail traders will probably have greater access to AI and ML as these technologies advance, giving them access to capabilities that were previously only available to institutional investors.

Cryptocurrencies' Increasing Impact The role of cryptocurrencies in international finance is expanding, as is their impact on currency trading. In addition to providing special trading opportunities, digital currencies like Ethereum (ETH) and Bitcoin (BTC) are occasionally employed as a hedge against conventional fiat currencies.

Crypto-Cross Pairs: In order to

enable traders to speculate on cryptocurrency fluctuations against major fiat currencies, many brokers now offer crypto-cross pairs, such as BTC/USD and ETH/EUR. Decentralized Finance (DeFi): Without the need for middlemen, DeFi platforms enable traders to lend, borrow, and exchange cryptocurrencies.

Decentralized exchanges (DEXs), which enable peer-to-peer forex trading and provide an alternative to conventional brokerages, have grown as a result of this.

Forex stablecoins include USDT (Tether) and USDC (USD Coin), which are based on fiat currencies and offer a reliable alternative to fiat money.

In times of market volatility, some traders turn to stablecoins as a haven.
As digital currencies become more widely accepted, their integration into the forex market may continue to expand.
Cryptocurrencies give forex traders other assets to diversify their portfolios.

Growing Utilization of High-Frequency and Algorithmic Trading High-frequency trading (HFT) and algorithmic trading are growing in popularity, especially as technology advances and becomes more accessible.

Speed and Latency Advancements: Faster order execution is now possible due to lower latency brought about by improvements in server infrastructure and network speeds.

HFT traders benefit from this, particularly in erratic markets. Algorithmic trading has the potential to enable automated market-making, in which algorithms set buy and sell orders based on the current market price.

This gives the forex market liquidity and makes it possible for other dealers to fulfill orders more quickly.

Scalability for Retail Traders: Individual traders now have access to some algorithmic tools thanks to the growth of retail-focused trading platforms and VPS hosting.

They can mimic the tactics of profitable algorithmic traders through "copy trading" or automate systems.

As technology develops and gives traders more tools for quick and effective trading, algorithmic trading is probably going to become even more important in the forex market.

Decentralized Exchanges and Blockchain Technology.

Blockchain technology's introduction of decentralized infrastructure, security, and transparency is having an effect on currency trading.

New methods of trading currencies without middlemen are provided by decentralized exchanges, or DEXs.

Security and Transparency:

The decentralized ledger of blockchain technology makes it possible to record transactions transparently, which lowers the risk of fraud.

Trust in the trading process may be strengthened by this more transparency, particularly in areas with lax regulatory monitoring. Decentralized Forex Trading: By offering peer-to-peer forex trading platforms, DEXs help consumers maintain control over their money and lessen their reliance on brokers. Although it is still in its infancy, decentralized forex trading might save expenses and provide traders greater freedom.

Smart Contracts: On the blockchain, smart contracts enable automatic, self-executing agreements.

They can, for instance, automatically conclude trades when certain criteria are satisfied, giving trading an additional degree of automation and dependability.

Blockchain technology could result in new decentralized solutions that transform currency trading as it develops further.

Increased Attention to Socially Responsible Trading and Sustainability Financial markets, especially forex trading, are being impacted by the growing popularity of environmental, social, and governance (ESG) concepts. A growing number of traders and investors are thinking about how long their investments will last. **ESG's Effect on Currency Values:** Investor confidence may be higher in currencies from nations that place a high priority on sustainability and social responsibility.

For example, a nation with stable economic conditions and robust environmental regulations may draw in foreign investment, which would boost its currency.

Socially Responsible Trading Platforms:

A number of trading platforms are providing forex tools that support socially responsible investing and incorporating ESG data.

This enables traders to make trading decisions based on their values.

Environmental Impact of Trading: As concerns about the effects of trading technologies on the environment grow, more brokers and platforms are trying to implement eco-friendly procedures, such as powering data centers with renewable energy.

A greater emphasis on ESG and sustainability could influence currency patterns and motivate traders to apply these ideas to their trading plans.

The Function of Advanced Analytics and Big.

Data Because they provide insights that were previously unavailable, big data and advanced analytics are becoming indispensable in forex trading.

Traders can assess risks, identify subtle market trends, and improve methods by examining huge datasets.

Sentiment Analysis from Big Data: A real-time picture of market sentiment can be obtained by analyzing enormous volumes of news and social media data.

For example, abrupt spikes in internet mentions of specific currencies could be a sign of impending volatility.

Predictive analytics: Sophisticated analytics systems are able to evaluate historical price changes and generate models that forecast future price movements.

Trend forecasting and risk assessment benefit greatly from predictive analytics.

Data Visualization:

Tools for data visualization assist traders in comprehending intricate market data.

Trends and correlations that might not be immediately apparent can be found using heatmaps, scatter plots, and other visual aids.

Big data will give traders better insights and increase the accuracy of their decision-making as data gathering and analysis methods improve.

Changing Regulatory Environment

Forex trading regulations are always changing to meet concerns about technology, fraud, and transparency. In the upcoming years, traders' and brokers' operations will probably be impacted by changes in the regulatory environment.

Enhanced Transparency.

Rules designed to promote transparency may mandate that brokers reveal more details, including risk disclosures, fees, and pricing strategies.

Traders will be able to make better selections as a result.

Stricter Leverage Restrictions: To safeguard retail traders, certain regions are enforcing stricter leverage limits.

Certain trading techniques may be impacted by lower leverage since it restricts profit possibilities while lowering risk exposure.

International Regulatory Cooperation:

In an effort to prevent fraud and guarantee ethical trading, regulatory organizations from all over the world are attempting to standardize forex trading laws.

This might result in more uniform regulations across many jurisdictions, enhancing trader safety everywhere.

Traders can stay compliant and be ready for developments that may affect their trading strategy by being aware of the regulatory environment.

The Development of Copy and Social Trading Platforms for social and copy trading, which let traders follow and imitate the tactics of more seasoned traders, are growing in popularity.

Copy Trading Platforms: By enabling traders to duplicate trades made by profitable traders, platforms such as eToro and ZuluTrade provide them the chance to learn from others and maybe make money.

easily learn forex trading by utilizing the experience of seasoned pros thanks to social and copy trading platforms.

The growth of social and copy trading is probably going to continue, increasing the accessibility, interaction, and instructional value of forex trading.

Possible Effects of Changes in Geopolitics Currency markets can be significantly impacted by geopolitical events including trade wars, international sanctions, and changes in economic alliances.

More and more forex traders are keeping an eye on these developments in order to modify their tactics.

Changing Economic Alliances: Nations are establishing new commercial alliances that have the potential to affect exchange rates. For example, the demand for currencies such as the Japanese yen or the Chinese yuan may be impacted by new trade agreements in Asia.

Currency values may be impacted by economic nationalism, which occurs when nations place a higher priority on their own sectors than on international trade.

For instance, nationalistic policies frequently come with trade restrictions and currency devaluations, which have an impact on forex markets.

Impact of Sanctions: Currency markets may be affected by sanctions on nations such as Russia or Iran, which can have an impact on both the sanctioned country and the international supply chains in which it is involved.

Traders can more accurately predict currency swings and make wise trading decisions if they closely monitor geopolitical happenings.

An overview of Chapter 12 Future trends in forex trading were examined in Chapter 12, which also included technological developments, the impact of cryptocurrencies, the promise of blockchain, and the changing regulatory environment.

The forex market is about to undergo major changes that will improve accessibility, efficiency, and trading prospects for traders thanks to new technologies like artificial intelligence (AI), big data, and algorithmic trading. By keeping up with these developments, traders will be more equipped to adjust to shifts, utilize new resources, and make calculated choices in a dynamic international market. We'll wrap off the following chapter with a review of the experience of FX trading, offering

Chapter 13

Final Thoughts and Upcoming Actions for Your Forex Adventure.

Examining Your Forex Experience A dynamic career path full of chances, difficulties, and ongoing education is provided by forex trading.

As this book draws to a close, it is important to pause and consider the fundamental concepts, methods, and resources that have been discussed. You now have a comprehensive understanding of what it takes to be successful in forex, from knowing the fundamentals and picking a broker to mastering sophisticated trading strategies and adjusting to emerging trends.

Forex demands perseverance, self-control, and a dedication to expansion; it is not a "get rich quick" scheme.

Every successful trader experiences a learning curve that includes victories, setbacks, and epiphanies. You will be well-equipped to handle the intricacies of the forex market and create a trading strategy that fits your objectives and risk tolerance if you remain rooted in the ideas covered in this book.

Creating a Growth Mentality
Long-term success in forex trading requires a growth mentality, which is the conviction that abilities and knowledge can be enhanced with time and effort.

This is how to cultivate it:
Consider Errors as Teaching Opportunities:
Every error teaches us something. Analyze losses, determine what went wrong, and use the knowledge gained to steer clear of similar blunders in the future rather than moping over them.
Establish Small, Achievable Goals: Divide your trading trip into manageable, realistic goals.

Incremental goals help you stay motivated and monitor your progress, whether your goal is to increase your win rate, learn a new tactic, or develop emotional discipline.

Continue to Learn and Be Curious: Since the forex market is always changing, keep an open mind to new ideas, tactics, and resources.

To keep informed and motivated, participate in trading communities, read articles, and attend webinars. By adopting a growth mentality, traders can develop the mental toughness necessary to succeed in the forex market and remain resilient in trying situations.

Creating a Trading Strategy for the Long Run.

You can approach forex trading with consistency and purpose by developing a long-term trading plan. It entails establishing precise goals, laying out plans, and creating guidelines that support your financial objectives.

<u>Identify Your Trading Style</u>: Choose between becoming a long-term investor, swing trader, or day trader. The time demands, tactics, and risk profiles of each style vary.

<u>Establish Specific Financial Objectives:</u>

Establish quantifiable, precise financial goals, such as milestones for account growth or a monthly return percentage.

Having specific goals helps you stay on track and gives you a standard by which to measure your progress.

<u>**Review and Modify Your Plan Frequently:**</u>

Trading tactics are subject to change as markets do. Review your trading strategy frequently and make any adjustments in light of your experiences, performance, and the state of the market.

Consistency requires a long-term plan, which keeps you on track and helps you avoid making snap decisions.

<u>**Establishing a Weekly and Daily Schedule.**</u>

By creating a trading routine, you can make sure that you are focused and prepared for every trading session.

Building sound trading habits and strengthening discipline require consistency.

<u>Daily Routine</u>: Examine open positions, examine economic calendars for significant events, and evaluate important currency pairings before each trading session. Making educated decisions and maintaining perspective are facilitated by a daily review.

<u>Weekly Review</u>.

Examine your journal entries, trades, and if you adhered to your plan and risk management guidelines each week.

You may address your shortcomings, pinpoint your strengths, and modify your strategy as necessary with the help of this weekly review.

A regular schedule promotes discipline, lessens emotional trading, and allows for steady advancement.

<u>Skill Development and Ongoing Education.</u>

Being knowledgeable is essential to remaining competitive and adaptable in the ever-evolving world of forex trading. additional Certifications and Courses.

As you acquire expertise, think about pursuing additional certifications or courses that address subjects like risk management, sophisticated technical analysis, or algorithmic trading.

Keeping Up with Market News: You may stay educated on the variables influencing currency markets by keeping up with events in the global economy and geopolitics.

You can keep ahead of the game with the use of trustworthy news sources, economic calendars, and FX research tools.

Learning from Other Traders: Social networks, online forums, and trading communities are excellent places to exchange ideas and gain knowledge from the experiences of other traders.

Interact with others to improve your tactics and acquire fresh viewpoints. Your trading abilities remain sharp thanks to ongoing education, which also helps you adjust to shifting market conditions.

Maintaining Motivation

Despite Setbacks Maintaining motivation is crucial for enduring the unavoidable ups and downs in forex trading, which can be difficult.

Enjoy Little Victories:

Whether you've learned a new skill or reached a monthly objective, acknowledge and enjoy your success. Little victories boost self-esteem and drive. Profits are important, but concentrating only on the bottom line can cause stress and emotional decision-making. Instead, concentrate on the process. Concentrate on controlling risks, making sure trades are executed correctly, and improving your approach.

Consistently using good practices will lead to profits.

<u>Seek Help When Needed</u>: Since trading can be lonely, don't be afraid to ask for help from mentors, trading organizations, or other traders.

You may maintain your motivation, optimism, and sense of groundedness by sharing your experiences.

You can stay consistent and overcome obstacles if you remain motivated through the highs and lows.

<u>Concluding Remarks</u> As you go with your forex journey, bear in mind these important guidelines:

<u>Patience is Key</u>: Those who are disciplined and patient are rewarded in forex trading.

You will make mistakes if you rush; instead, wait for possibilities to present themselves based on your research and approach.

<u>Remain Disciplined</u>: The foundation of profitable trading is discipline. Always stick to your trading strategy, observe risk management guidelines, and refrain from making rash, emotionally motivated deals. <u>Be Flexible</u>: Because the forex market is ever-changing, flexibility is crucial. Maintain an open mind, keep abreast of developments in technology and trends, and modify your tactics as needed.

<u>Invest in Yourself</u>: Putting money into yourself is the finest thing you can do.

Include personal growth, mental toughness, and ongoing education in your trading regimen.

You may make forex trading a fulfilling endeavor that supports both your financial objectives and personal development if you have the necessary perseverance, self-control, and dedication to learning.

An overview of Chapter 13 A thorough wrap-up of the book was given in Chapter 13, which urged traders to consider their forex experience, cultivate a growth attitude, and create a long-term trading strategy. Traders can successfully manage the difficulties of the forex market and attain long-term success by establishing routines, focusing on constant development, and committing to ongoing education. Keep in mind that forex trading is as much about resilience and personal development as it is about technical expertise, and that a methodical, flexible approach will put you on the road to sustained success. I wish you well as you embark on your forex trading adventure!

www.ingramcontent.com/pod-product-compliance
Lightning Source LLC
Chambersburg PA
CBHW071020240526
45469CB00006BD/2004